LIVING THINGS

MARLA CONN

Rourke
Educational Media
A Division of Carson Dellosa Education

rourkeeducationalmedia.com

Photo Glossary

bat

bee

cat

snail

tree

whale

High Frequency Words:
- a
- is
- living
- thing

A tree is a living thing.

tree

A **bee** is a living thing.

bee

A **cat** is a living thing.

cat

A **bat** is a living thing.

bat

11

A **snail** is a living thing.

snail

13

A **whale** is a living thing.

whale

Activity

1. Name all of the living things in the story.
2. Create a main idea and details chart on a separate piece of paper.

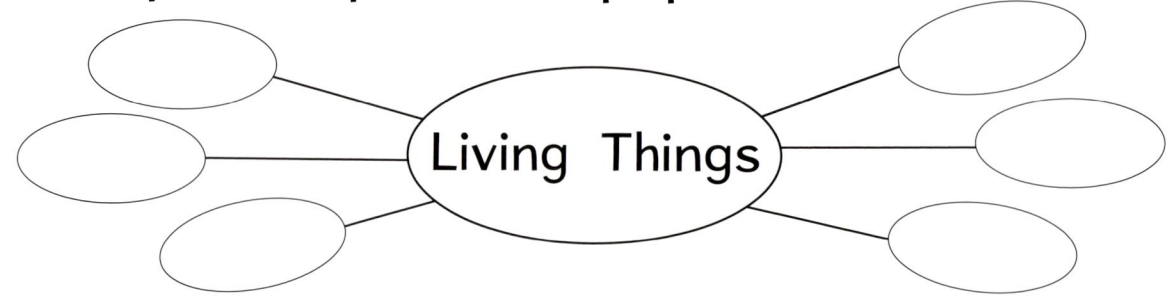

```
       ◯                    ◯
        \                  /
   ◯----( Living Things )----◯
        /                  \
       ◯                    ◯
```

3. What do all of the living things in the story have in common?
4. How are living things different?
5. Find the rhyming words from the story- c**at**-b**at**, wh**ale**- sn**ail**, tr**ee**-b**ee**
6. Think of a living thing that rhymes with cat and bat. Draw a picture and write a sentence.